Math on the Job

Math at the Airport

Tracey Steffora

Heinemann
LIBRARY
Chicago, Illinois

Edited by Dan Nunn and Abby Colich
Designed by Victoria Allen
Picture research by Tracy Cummins
Production control by Vicki Fitzgerald

Printed and bound in China by Leo Paper Group

15 14 13 12
10 9 8 7 6 5 4 3 2 1

Library of Congress Cataloging-in-Publication Data
Steffora, Tracey.
  Math at the airport / Tracey Steffora.
    p. cm.—(Math on the job)
  Includes index.
  ISBN 978-1-4329-7151-9 (hb)—ISBN 978-1-4329-7158-8 (pb)
  1. Airports—Juvenile literature. 2. Mathematics—Juvenile literature. I. Title.

TL725.15.S74 2013
513—dc23   2012013370

Acknowledgments
The author and publishers are grateful to the following for permission to reproduce copyright material: Alamy: p. 14 (© Jim West); Corbis: pp. 15 (© Robert Maass); dreamstime: p. 21 (Fintastique); Getty Images: pp. 6 (Jupiterimages), 9 (Lester Lefkowitz), 10 (Digital Vision),11 (Andreas Koerner), 16 (Thinkstock), 18 (Karen Moskowitz), 23a (Jupiterimages); iStockphoto: pp. 5 (© Gene Chutka), 12 (© bojan fatur), 17 (© Gene Chutka), 19 (© mayo5); Shutterstock: pp. 4 (yxm2008), 7 (Remzi), 8 (Lisa S.), 13 (Lars Christensen), 20 (Eric Gevaert), 23b (Eric Gevaert).

Front cover photograph of a pilot sitting at the controls of a commercial airplane reproduced with permission from Getty Images/ Digital Vision/ James Lauritz.

Back cover photograph of a ground controller on a runway reproduced with permission from iStockphoto (© mayo5).

The publishers would like to thank Andy Colich for his invaluable help in the preparation of this book.

Every effort has been made to contact copyright holders of any material reproduced in this book. Any omissions will be rectified in subsequent printings if notice is given to the publisher.

Contents

Math at the Airport

Many people work at the airport.

Many people use math at
the airport.

Counting

flight attendant

The flight attendant counts tickets.

The flight attendant
counts passengers.

baggage handler

The baggage handler counts bags.

How many bags can you count?

(answer on page 22)

Measuring

pilot

The pilot flies the plane.

how fast

The pilot measures how fast.

how high

The pilot measures how high.

plane

tree

Which is higher? The plane or the tree? (answer on page 22)

Shape and Size

screener

The screener looks at bags.

x-ray

The screener looks at the shape
of things.

The flight attendant looks at bags.
Some bags are large.

Some bags are small. Is this bag large or small? (answer on page 22)

Time

ground controller

The ground controller tells a plane when to move.

ground controller

The ground controller tells a plane when to stop.

The air controller tells a plane
when to fly.

DEPARTURES

LOS ANGELES	7:20
SEATTLE	7:40
BOSTON	8:10
CHICAGO	8:30
NEW YORK	9:00
MIAMI	9:15
HOUSTON	9:50
DENVER	10:15

What time does the plane fly to New York? (answer on page 22)

Answers

page 9: There are five bags.

page 13: The plane is higher than the tree.

page 17: The bag is small.

page 21: The plane flies to New York at 9:00.

Picture Glossary

ticket paper that shows you have paid for something

air controller person who tells the pilot when to fly the plane

23

Index

Notes for parents and teachers
Math is a way that we make sense of the world around us. For the young child, this includes recognizing similarities and differences, classifying objects, recognizing shapes and patterns, developing number sense, and using simple measurement skills.

Before reading
Connect with what children know.
Discuss types of transportation and identify that one way we can travel is by airplane. Allow children to share any experiences they have had at the airport and on an airplane and encourage them to name as many workers as they can.

After reading
Build upon children's curiosity and desire to explore.
With children, look at the photos of the cockpit and discuss how pilots use different instruments of measurement. Some children will be interested to learn that an altimeter tells the distance the plane is off the ground and an airspeed indicator tells the pilot how fast they are flying through the air.

In the gym or on the playground, demonstrate the importance of an air traffic controller by having one child be an "air traffic controller" while other children wait for directions to "take off." First have the controller count to 10 between telling individual children to "take off" (walking a single line). Then have them count to 2. Discuss how the distance between "planes" changes depending on when the controller tells them to take off.